AN ABERGAVENNY SONS' POETRY AND SKETCHES

AN ABERGAVENNY SONS' POETRY AND SKETCHES

by

Glyn Harris

P. M. Heaton Publishing
Abergavenny, Gwent
Great Britain.
1994

ISBN 1 872006 02 7

Published by P.M. Heaton Publishing, Abergavenny, Gwent. NP7 9UH
Printed by B & N Printers, Abergavenny, Gwent. NP7 5HE
Typesetting by Innerspace Design, Leominster, Herefordshire. HR6 8EP

CONTENTS

INTRODUCTION

I was brought up in Tudor street, Abergavenny, where all were poor in possessions, but happily rich in experience and friendship, which comes of living in a closely - knit community.

When I was three years old my family identified my leaning towards art. At that time I had started sketching horses as they passed through the street.

Having embarked on my working life, I have always enjoyed sketching and painting, particularly those things which have given me most pleasure. Horses and people rank among my favourites.

I am pleased to be able to produce this book containing a selection of my poems and sketches. A wide variety of subjects are covered, but I have endeavoured to feature 'people' and themes from both sides of the Atlantic. Hence the mixture of Country and Western, together with Sybil, Grandad, Sister Mary Teresa and others.

I hope that readers get as much pleasure from this book as I have had in compiling it.

Glyn Harris
October, 1994

Abergavenny

ABERGAVENNY

Once it was a 'Celtic' land
Then conquering Romans claimed
Green Velvet is this 'Vale of Usk'.
'Gobannium' they named
The Welsh, they had a difference
They said it's called Y-fenni
When the Normans broke our language up
We settled for 'Abergavenny'.

This vale has had it's noble Lords
Herbert, Hastings, Nevill
And the devious DeBroase
Whom Welshmen called the 'Devil'.
A saint lived here, not too far back
Courageous Father Baker
Who preached the 'wrong' religion
They dispatched him to his maker.

Industrialists, they've had their turn
Fine steel, hewn from the Blorenge
Hammers thundered, day and night
The skies lit, sunset orange.
You'd never guess it now, of course
The dramroads cloaked in moss
Furnaces, once fed by trees
At mother natures loss.

Still living in some memories
Abodes, with half-sty door
Like Tudor, Castle, Mill Street
All gone, alas, no more
Many wish to dwell here
Others need to roam
You can give it all the names you want
To me it's known as 'home'.

Her clothes are made of heavy tweed, her face be like a toad

SYBIL

There's a woman in our village
with whom you dare not quibble
She weighs around three hundred pounds
wears boots, her name is Sybil.
Her clothes are made of heavy tweed
her face be like a toad
and where she spits her 'bacci' out
it burns holes in the road.

Sybil never went to school
she wasn't very clever
She couldn't read 'BEWARE THE BULL'
which came at her hell for leather.
"Is she hurt!" her friends all cried
"No! Only hurt her pride!"
But the farmers got it on him
'cos the bull 'as nearly died.

We gathered in the church one day
one of the boys was getting wed
"D'you know of any impediment?"
The Vicar he had read.
"I know of one!" called Sybil
"That man that's by her side
owes me four pints of cider
so he can't afford a bride!"

Sybil mucked in with the lads
to help with the hay making
By gosh! We had a thirst on
'cos the sun was really baking.
The farmer brought rough cider
that made our throats turn raw
Sybil drank the barrel dry
Burped! then asked for more!

She left the pub on one dark night
Leapt on by three muggers
They were going to beat our Sybil up
Silly little buggers!
She whirled the one around her head
looked like a helicopter
and kicked the others half to death
'til the local copper stopped her.

Rugger team turned up one night
By gosh! They all looked tough
And when they had the booze in them
they didn't half get rough.
They laid the boys out in the lounge
But, in the bar, they did encroach
So Sybil 'flattened' the lot of them
and ripped the engine out of their coach.

If you see our Sybil out
Wave and show you're friend
'cos when you're friends with Sybil
She's with you to the end.
You'll see her taking trekkers out
She's the one who sits much higher
'Cos the only horse to take her weight
is an eighteen two hands shire!

But the farmers got it on him 'cos the bull 'as nearly died

was an indian, lean and old

THE SPIRIT OF OLD CHIEF IRONFACE

The time was 'round high noon
and the month was 'flaming June'
when the bandits raided town.
Every one a real hard case
started shooting up the place
Didn't give us a chance to turn around.

In no time at all
they'd had themselves a ball,
drinking all the whisky and the wine.
Honest people stayed at home
afraid to God darn roam
as from now the town was on the decline.

Bandits sang their filthy tunes
in one of the saloons
A place they cared to call H.Q.
Then, tiring of their games
they started smashing the remains
'mongst them relics of the long gone Sioux.

They broke tomahawks
to howls of jeers and squawks
Ripped medicine beads and indian leathers.
But they sure did bring on grief
when they grabbed a mighty chief's
headdress made of eagle feathers.

The sky was suddenly blacked
Thunder and lightening cracked
Funny for that time of year.
Then, we heard the hums
of distant war drums
and those bad mens eyes, they sure showed fear.

The doors flew open wide
and there stood outside
was an indian, lean and old.
Although tired and boney
t'was a real man, no phoney
and he made their blood run cold.

Having got over the shock
those louts started to mock
that dignified old brave.
When he swiftly pulled his bow
and let a dozen arrows go
and those hoodlums started to rave.

Well, the bullets flew
but they seemed to go through
the ducking, weaving warrior.
Every bandit died
some they whimpered, some they cried
but, they sure ended up the sorrier.

Gunsmoke, swirled around
and the indian found
the relic eagle feathers.
Then, he put them on
and in a flash was gone
on a horse as lean and tough as leather.

At last someone spoke out
t'was an old indian scout
said he knew the Chief, knew him well.
Met him fifty years before
after some great indian war
Condemned, in an army prison cell.

The scout said t'was 'Ironface'
and he'd begged the great white race
not to hang him for his soul would wander round.
Then he asked me, I was near
if I'd bury him back here
You see, this town's on an old indian burial ground.

But, we all turned traitors
when urged on by agitators
Hung him, so his soul'd forever wander.
So I advise you all get out!
now old Ironface is about
'Cos you see, he's in the hills out yonder.

Well, it's a ghost town now
and with a ghost you can't pow-pow
and the town belongs to old Chief Ironface.
He guards his peoples graves
I know you think I rant and rave
But, listen here! Don't go near the God damned place.

and the indian found the relic eagle feathers

Crying in my whisky

Just a Sunset Cowboy
    Autumn of my days
Rode the Rodeo circuit
    Never changed my ways
Now! My mind a 'wanders
    And my body aches
Drinking brings no pleasure
    Just gives me the 'shakes'
Once, I was a champion
    Fear! I never knew
Dollars! I earnt plenty
    But! The lot I blew
Now! Just a Sunset Cowboy
    Autumn of my days
Rode the Rodeo circuit
    Never changed my ways
Once! I had a sweet wife
    Drove her near insane
Every bone that I broke
    She lived with the pain
Now! Sunset comes to greet me
    I can't stand daylight
'Neon' suits me better
    Cos I'm not a pretty sight
Just a Sunset Cowboy
    Left with no more fight
Crying in my whisky
    Get me through another night.

Tudor Street

THE END OF OLD TUDOR STREET

Born into a wartorn world
Rat infested slum
Crumbling homes and poverty
What had we become?

Families crammed in tiny homes
'Sardines' in a bed
Good enough! For them! some thought
God! We were misread!

Most of us were spotless clean
Fighting all the odds
Governments who'd kept us down
Were the really rotten sods.

Limbless tramps sometimes passed through
Slept in Derelicts
Were they industrial accidents?
Or were they wartime wrecks?

Some could play accordions
I remember one, a trumpet
How the people fussed them
With pennies and hot crumpet.

Beckit Holland kept his horses
Proud actions, stepping light
I'd rush inside to draw them
'Cos I'd ne'er seen such a sight.

At 'Tudor House' dwelt Ginny Jones
A lady well respected
If you ever needed any clothes
She'd see you weren't neglected.

Secondhand, but neat and clean
For the workplace, or a ball
Suits and shoes, jackets too
For next to now't at all.

Established as 'Removal Man'
Our very own Bob 'Star'
Well known at the furniture sales
He carried near and far.

Sideboards, chairs and wardrobes
If you found you couldn't cope
and the 'Magic' was he did it all
with an ancient pram and rope.

Struggling with his heavy load
Some balanced precariously
And to his consternation
Kids laughed hilariously.

Double beds I think were worst
They made him quite frustrated
But, once customers passed their 'tanners' on
He went on his way 'elated'.

We all knew he lived in squalor,
Taken for granted by 'The Street'
But admit it now, jogged memory
Your heart just lept a beat.

Old Tudor had it's little shops
Which we'd patronise in turn
So they each could make a shilling
For a 'crust' they had to earn.

Proud; were working menfolk
Shame; if on the dole
But, for all their degradation
No-one harmed a soul.

Wars-end brought celebration
Wireless's would 'sing'
Jolson crooning 'mammy'
Ballads groaned by 'Bing'.

Laughter filled the 'Kings Arms'
And as the booze was sunk
'Bluebirds over Dover'
On the lips of all who drunk.

Churchill was the hero
"Man who won the war!"
Atlee got our Labour Vote
When canvassed at the door.

I really ought to mention,
That the leader of my 'gang'
T'was a girl as tough as leather
And she fought just like a man.

Teeth like a 'Rotweiller'
If another street should fight
I'm glad she was on our side
She'd put 'em all to 'flight'.

Where she is today of course
I'd simply have to guess
But, if she's half the girl she used to be
She commands the S.A.S.

We had our share of heaven
On a Sunday I recall
It was the annual outing
To Barry or Porthcawl.

The only day we wore new clothes
For we had to look quite 'posh'
Stood up in an old tin bath
And take a real good wash!

'Tudor' supplied footballers
To represent the town.
Some, well worth a mention
Brought us great renown.

Kenny Neil at number four
In defence showed super promise
Terry Hodges, Danny Connell
and also Colin Thomas.

If you pestered me to make a choice
It would be a close decision
But another played for Cardiff,
Danny McCarthy, first division.

Two Bryns' became quite famous
Bryn Yemm, Celebrity
Bryn Seabourne, pinnacle of brains
Oxford University.

Jimmy Hill was our old Mayor
and later, his son Ray
Peter Madden, Newmarket 'Jock'
Yes, 'Tudor' had it's day.

Well! Progress comes to everyone
You can't stand in the way
Old Tudor Street is flattened
You can't see it today.

Upon the ground, they've built the dole
And new Police Station
Which, could the Ghosts speak from the past
They'd be filled with indignation

Some say "it was our heritage"
Old houses, well worth saving
With character and beauty
Like Stratford-upon-Avon

Too Late! Now, the deed is done
We've gone our different way
But all hold our opinion
Right, wrong! Just who can say?

I only know that those of us
Whose left, when e'er we meet
The greeting has a warmly 'glow'
'Cos we're from Tudor Street.

It came way back from Norman times
When Tudors ruled, the main street
now smelted into history
The 'Never-come-again' Street.

All who reads my story
By now, will comprehend
That the one's who felt the greater loss
lived there right at the end.

Though it's many years ago
I still miss those friendly faces
Yet I've since had lovely neighbours
And, lived in some nice places.

I think it was the atmosphere
Of welcome open doors
Or unity thats' brought about
By poverty and wars.

All flash across the line

THE RACING GAME

Nostrils flaring, flashing eyes
Blood rushing through their veins
Thoroughbreds pushed into stalls
Handlers heaves and strains
Nerves a tingling, bets are 'on'
Send them on their way
Starter on his rostrum
Lets hope there's no delay
All is well! All are in!
Now! Release the gate!
Horses flying through the air
"Jockeys'! Keep them straight!"
Hear the hooves a pounding
The race can now begin
Coloured silks speed up the course
Only one can win
Round the bend, "hold the rails"
Never give remission
Riders jostling in the pack
Fighting for position
Comes the final furlong
Hear the Grandstand roar
Horses getting weary
Riders ask for more
Carson drives into the lead
Followed by Dettori
Piggot makes a final burst
Who will take the glory?
Eddery has joined the fray
All flash across the line
Who the hell has won it?
Your guess is good as mine!
Announcer blasts across the crowd

There'll be a "photograph"
Bookies stare and punters dream
But no one wants to laugh
At last! we know the outcome
Everyone's alert!
Someone has won a fortune
Anothers 'lost his shirt'
I hope your nerves can hold out
And you can stick the pace
Its going to be a long day
That was only the first race!

THE SLIMMERS DILEMMA

At last! I'm down to eight stone two
I'm feeling really great!
I'm going home to Bertie
Going to put the record straight.

I've been a pain, to live with
It's the diet, can't you see!
He's had to go through sheer hell
But he's forgiven me.

I've burnt up all my calories
And his bank balance too!
Cos my old clothes wouldn't' fit me
So I've had to buy all new.

For months I'm on this diet
Cos I really had to slim
And now I'm oh so slender
I've just worked out in the gym.

I've melted in the Turkish bath
Lived off celery and lettuce
You girls know what I've been through
We get this slimmers fetish.

Berts had to live off porridge
Nuts 'n' cabbage, grapes 'n' carrot
When I left our home at teatime
He looked sicker than a parrot!

Hello! Whats in the kitchen?
Theres a note thats left for me
It's from my dearest Bertie
Now what can it be?

He's left me for another!
Surely its a bluff!
Says he'd have more fun in prison
And he's finally had enough.

He's left me for that Barbara
Says she's cuddly and she's fat
Why, she's built just like an elephant,
The dirty rotten rat!

I've tortured myself physically
And all of it for him
Where's the ruddy frying pan
I must be ruddy dim.

Get the eggs 'n' chips on
Cut me a lump of cheese
Give me back my fat old hips
And bulges at the knees!

Chuck a lump of suet in
Blow the grapes 'n' fig
I want to look like Barbara
The great big fat old pig!

Get the eggs 'n' chips on

Yet life goes on without you

THE LEAVING OF MY LOVE

Life goes on without you
Dawn breaks yet again
But the days that you have left me
Will never be the same.

I can see you always
Feel you in the breeze
Everywhere I hear you
Like songbirds in the trees.

Yet life goes on without you
Night time seems so long
Day brings peoples laughter
But I feel I don't belong.

Sadness you have left me
In my heart and soul
My fault you have left me
Now! I must pay the toll.

Dust that leaves you dry

SWEETWATER 'GAL'

Sun that burns your eyes out
Dust that leaves you dry
Sweetwater gal on my mind
My heart heaves a sigh
There, a girls awaiting
Waiting just for me
And as I ride this desert trail
Like a mirage, her I see
Cattle! Move your hides on
Doggys! Don't you roam
Sweetwater gal's a calling
Calling me back home
Chuckwagon grub is wholesome
Get's you through the day
But, theres nothing like home-cooking
Done Sweetwater way.

"Hello, Handsome Cowboy!"

I was just turned eighteen
When the Circus came to town
Well paid from a cattle drive
I decided to look around
Nothing took my interest
Only one thing caught my eye
T'was a dark bespangled lady
And she winked as I walked by.

"Hello! Handsome Cowboy!
Is it pleasure that you seek?"
And she moved her body in a way
That made my knees go weak.
Her skirt was high, her blouse was low,
She wore that Eastern scent
I didn't walk, I kind'a run
As she called me to her tent.

Inside there was a lonely man
She called him 'Uncle Ben'
Little did I realise
I was in the 'Lions Den'
"I'll change to something comfortable
I'll be back bye'n'bye
You two play cards while I'm gone"
First she opened a bottle of Rye.

Well! The stakes were low, so I had a 'go'
And my luck was really in
No matter how he shuffled those cards
This guy just couldn't win
By this time the girl returned
In a gown of powder blue
And as she stood against the light
The dress I could see straight through.

"Up the stakes?" Said 'Uncle Ben'
"Go on? I must insist!"
And the way that he was losing
T'was a chance I couldn't resist
"Well done! Handsome Cowboy!
I like a man thats risky!"
And the girl leaned low, behind me now
And refilled my glass with whisky.

I may have been wrong, but 'Uncle Ben'
Seemed to deal the cards much quicker
In an hour or so, my money had gone
And so had all the liquor
"Time to go, young Cowboy!"
'Uncle Ben' spoke mighty rough
And as he grabbed me by my shirt
Two cards fell from his cuff.

"Dirty cheat!" I began to bleat
And my fist crashed to his jaw
But, I was hit hard from behind
And I remember no more
Well! It was dawn when I came to
It's a hell of a taste, defeat
No tent was there, cause they were gone
They sure found me 'easy meat'.

O.K! Circus Lady
You made me out a clown
But, one day soon, we'll meet again
In some other cattle town
and I'll learn fast, and I'll move quick
And this you'd better believe,
That like that 'card shark' with you
I'll have a few tricks up my sleeve.

And my fist crashed to his jaw

while we were fighting for a girl, McBain was fighting them off!

"M^C BAIN"

Way down, in a Southern town,
I was born and bred.
Our neighbour had an only boy,
Who's hair was a shock of red.
Well! As kids he issued challenges,
Time and time again.
We took 'em up, but we couldn't win,
Against this boy called Jim Mc Bain.

Real brainy was this red haired boy,
Clever at his schools.
No matter what the lessons,
He made us all look fools.
When it came to fighting,
Didn't stand much chance,
McBain was like 'greased lightning'
And we ended on our pants.

As time went by, as we grew up,
McBain he sure grew bigger
He made us look a 'weedy' lot
And sometimes he would snigger.
When we started Cowboy work,
You'd hear the swearing and the 'damns'
At Mustangs that had thrown us
For McBain they came like lambs.

At courting, we were gentlemen,
And our hat's we'd doff
And while we were fighting for a girl,
McBain was fighting them off!
My wife was acting strangely,
And sometimes off she'd sneak
I found her in McBains arms
And we'd only been married a week!

I lived alone when my country called
And off I went to war
In a way, I was kind'a glad
I thought I'd see McBain no more
I returned with bullet wounds
On my face I had a dent
McBain returned with medals
A 'walking monument'.

Times got hard, work was scarce,
Most of us were poor.
McBain invested heavily,
His wealth grew more and more.
I turned alcoholic,
And no one seemed to care,
McBain put up for office,
And they voted him the mayor.

I've had enough of my home town,
And enough of Jim McBain.
I've packed my bags and sold my horse,
I'm catching the next train.
Next time this town sees me,
I'll be in my coffin,
"McBain! You cheated somewhere!
No guy should win that often".

I've had enough of my home town

Rest in peace dear Grandad

"HELLO, GRANDAD!"

Hello, Grandad, longtime gone,
I'm feeling so confused
I've got some tales to tell you
Don't think you'll be amused
Rest in Peace dear Grandad
Your not missing a thing
What families gained 'on roundabout'
Some lose out on 'the swing'.

Remember? Dear Grandad,
Those times we went to war
I fought mine up in Spitfires
You fought yours on the floor
We gave this generation
Victory in their laps
Now, guess who leads in peacetime?
The Germans and the Japs!

D'know? Dear Grandad
They've been up to the moon
Yet half the world's still starving
And inflation has ballooned
Wages have gone up tenfold
Yet life don't get no better
When I hear from sister, Margi
Always tears in her letter.

Do you know dear Grandad
We've got thugs called 'muggers'
Often beats old people up
Nasty little 'buggers'
Last year, attacked and robbed me
Pinned me to a door
And on the vests of two of them, said
"Make love! Don't make War!"

Another thing, dear Grandad
Everyone's got 'tele'
And every night without a miss
They show bottoms, breasts and belly
It's not love they're on about
Usually just plain sex!
This generation, Grandad
Will end up nervous wrecks.

Honestly! dear Grandad
Wouldn't recognise our 'Locals'
You mustn't speak at Bingo
Or you can't, for groups 'n' vocals
'Rolling Stones' and 'Beatles'
Played so loud your eardrums 'ring'
And theres signs displayed for customers
"You're not allowed to sing".

Remember? Mrs Wilkinson
Brought ten kids up alone
Now, her childrens all got cars
And all of them's got 'phone'
Last week she cracked up from the stress
Her minds began to roam
It's 'inconvenient' to her kids
So they put her in a 'home'.

D'you know what? Dear Grandad
I'm a Grandad too.
Midst lots of smiling faces
And some look just like you.
So, cheerio! Dear Grandad
To you, my hat I doff
I remembered all you taught me
And picked up where you left off.

Remember? Mrs. Wilkinson brought ten kids up alone

And scar my lovely features

PLIGHT OF MOTHER EARTH

Hello! Yes, you, the human race,
Mother nature calling.
I want some urgent answers,
'Cos your habits are appalling.
You think you're so superior,
Above all other creatures,
Yet, you don't see them abuse me,
And scar my lovely features.
Your violence, your greedy ways,
Your pollution and your sinning,
All started with that Adam and Eve,
Right from the beginning.
And all that high technology,
Has only made you worse,
Instead of progressing with the times,
You've gone into reverse.
You drill my precious innards,
For diamonds, gold and oil,
Then chemicals and bombs are dropped,
That contaminate my soil.
I warn you! I won't take much more,
I'll give one almighty blow!
And shoot you all off into space,
Then where will you go?
So, get your act together,
Look around and see,
That so-called inferior creatures,
Are in perfect harmony.

Receive the crowds applause

THE GYPSY QUEEN

Matador! So lithe and bold
All grace, with cape and sword
All ladies eyes upon you
They see you're never bored

Now! In all your triumph
Too late! My eyes you've seen
In my web you're tangled
You're mine! The Gypsy Queens.

Tonight my arms enfold you
You'll feel love you've never known
For the sun has sent me passion
And the moon will hold back dawn.

My heart is flame, my blade cold steel
Emotions ruled by passion
So eyes off! Handsome matador
Off! Ladies of high fashion.

Kill your bulls, oh matador
Receive the crowds applause
But, till Gypsy Queen discards you
You're ruled by gypsy laws.

She whispers that she loves me

SEA WITCH

Summer sun, summer wine
White foam on lonely beaches
Hazy head, yet feeling fine
For another bottle reaches.

Heavy head, heavy eyes
Gentle breezes sighing
Golden sands that nestles me
Sleep! My mind is crying.

Eyelids flicker, opens wide
How long have I been here?
Senses speak, you're not alone
A figures standing near.

Tall, slender creature, golden tanned
Now she stands above me
Faultless features, reaches out
She whispers that she loves me.

Full petal lips, deep violet eyes
My mind and soul caresses
And just to tantalise me more
Slowly she undresses.

Wondrous feelings, touch the sun
My mind is really 'blown'
My visions psychedelic
This bird has really flown.

Bodies writhing, souls are claimed
Each, we each explore
Burn each other with our love
Yet we cry out for more.

Slowly I float back to earth
On me she has first claim
She stands against the evening light
Silhouetted, sunset flame.

"Sea Witch" am I! Oh mortal man
Oceans do I roam!'
And slowly she glides from my reach
Beneath the raging foam.

"Sea Witch!" Which sea?
Tell me do you roam?
Tantalising sailors
Always from far flung home.

I see you witch, with outstretched arms
Out there you beckon me
I'll be immortal, just like you
And I walk into the sea.

A body washed up on the beach
His death a mystery
He had so much to live for
The world was his to see.

No marks upon his body
No motives, not a trace!
But, how on earth could any man die
With such a smile upon his face?

I see you witch, with out-stretched arms, out there you beckon me.

Gateway to Wales

St.Michaels' Mount brings morning light
Sun lifting from the East
Then rises yet across the vale
Like fresh bread laced with yeast
Floating in a cobalt sky
Burning summer fields
Barley, wheat smile in reply
Improving farmers yields
Meandering people walk in the 'Usk'
Away from all the hassle
Sleepy cows find sheltering trees
Overlooked by Norman castle
In autumn stroll St. Mary's vale
Carpet of golden leaves
Tread the stream o'er ancient stones
As in and out it weaves
Winter brings the snowcapped hills
Seven! Just like Rome
Whence, Emperors dispatched brave men
To 'win' this second home
In springtime daffodils abound
Like arrows in a quiver
Martins' nest in sandy banks
Spaced out along the river
This precious land, this earth I love
Heathered hills and velvet vales
I comprehend the reasons why
You're called 'Gateway to Wales.

Loose another mustang under me

LOOSE ANOTHER MUSTANG UNDER ME!

Loose another mustang under me
Theres no other life I can see
I'll have my up'n'downs
Broken bones and broken crowns
But, loose another mustang under me.

Let another calf out of that pen
Watch me rope'n'tie him, count to ten
Send out that long horned steer
Then all of you stand clear
And loose another mustang under me.

Rodeo riding is my only life
One night stands for me, but not a wife
Give me a brahmer bull
And my life is full
Then loose another mustang under me.

Cowboy, just open up my shute
I'll show you how to handle that brute
Then, remember my name well
For your kids you'll want to tell
Then loose another mustang under me.

Flying on her moped

SISTER MARY TERESA

I've know her since I was a child
She's always been the same
So happy and so cheerful
As if lifes just a game.

Visits sick and healthy
Talks to rich and poor
Uplifting all their spirits
Who could ask for more?

Flying on her moped
All over Abergavenny
If anyone could please you more
I can't think of any!

A treasure from old Ireland
Who crosses all divides
Who brings the sun on rainy days
And always sees both sides.

I've seen her at a woman's bed
With a trinket that she's bought her
Giving her the will to live
Young enough to be her daughter.

I wouldn't like to guess her age
Times never brought complaint
At crosses that I'm sure she's bore
She really is a Saint.

She'll be so pleased to see you
And say "You're looking fine"
Well! Sister Mary Teresa
The pleasures been all mine.

Take me down to the waters, Lord

TAKE ME DOWN TO THE WATERS, LORD

Take me down to the waters, Lord,
Heal my body, cleanse my soul,
Rebaptize with your sacred oils,
Make me pure again and whole.

We are born with sweet innocence
Which we lose along the way,
Skys' are blue, rivers clear, my Lord,
Without you they'd turn to grey.

I have taken many roads in life,
Some were crooked and untrue,
I have wandered into darkness, Lord
Shine the light that leads to You!

Give me faith! make me strong again,
I have strayed off from Your flock,
Holy Shepherd take me to your fold,
To your home thats built on rock.

Take me down to the waters, Lord,
Heal my body, cleanse my soul,
Rid me of my secret fears, Lord
Make me pure again and whole.

P. M. HEATON PUBLISHING
OF ABERGAVENNY

TELEPHONE: 0873 840668

PUBLISHERS OF SHIPPING, TRANSPORT AND LOCAL BOOKS.

Always interested in considering local author's work.